PENGUIN  CLASSICS

MY SHAMELESS HEART

Amaru was a Sanskrit poet who probably wrote around the ninth century. Although virtually nothing is known about his life, his *Amaru Shatakam* is one of the most admired collections of love lyrics in the Sanskrit language. Amaru's poetic style has been appreciated through the centuries for conveying so much sentiment in a single stanza that each appears like a whole poem.

Aditya Narayan Dhairyasheel Haksar is a well-known translator of Sanskrit classics. A long-time career diplomat, he served as the Indian high commissioner in Kenya and the Seychelles, as a minister in the United States and as an ambassador in Portugal and Yugoslavia. His translations from the Sanskrit include *Hitopadesa*, *Simhasana Dvatrimsika*, *Subhashitavali*, *Kama Sutra*, *The Courtesan's Keeper*, *Raghuvamsam* and most recently *Chanakya Niti*, all published in Penguin Classics.

My Shameless Heart

Love Lyrics of
Amaru Shatakam

Translated from the original Sanskrit by

A.N.D. Haksar

PENGUIN BOOKS

An imprint of Penguin Random House

PENGUIN BOOKS

USA | Canada | UK | Ireland | Australia
New Zealand | India | South Africa | China

Penguin Books is part of the Penguin Random House group of companies
whose addresses can be found at global.penguinrandomhouse.com

Published by Penguin Random House India Pvt. Ltd
7th Floor, Infinity Tower C, DLF Cyber City,
Gurgaon 122 002, Haryana, India

First published in Penguin Books by Penguin Random House India 2021

Copyright © A.N.D. Haksar 2021

ISBN 9780143450177

Typeset in Adobe Garamond Pro by Manipal Technologies Limited, Manipal
Printed at Replika Press Pvt. Ltd, India

www.penguin.co.in

P.M.S.

For
B.
With love

Contents

Introduction

The Sanskrit term *shatakam* indicates quantity, of about a hundred. *Amaru Shatakam,* with its that many colourful love lyrics, is one of the best known and highly regarded such works from the world of Sanskrit literature. This reputation has now existed in that literature's own record since over a thousand years. It has also been recognized in the Western world during the last century.

The earliest reference to this work, so far known, is from the ninth century commentary *Dhvanyaloka* (III.7), by the famous Sanskrit critic Anandavardhana of Kashmir (c. 850 AD). In his words as translated, 'Amaru proves that a poet can, in a single stanza, convey so much sentiment that each appears like a whole poem.'[1] Vamana, an earlier scholar statesman, also from Kashmir (c. 800 AD), has quoted some verses of Amaru in his own work, but without naming him.[2]

The oldest existing recension of *Amaru Shatakam*[3] was made and commented on by Arjuna Varma Deva (c. 1215 AD), a princely descendent of the celebrated scholar-king Bhoja from central India. Much respected, it is still in use, including by this translator. It has 102 verses with some others, later added by its editor in an appendix drawn from subsequent collections. Half a dozen of these are also included in the present translation. Other recensions date from the succeeding centuries.[4] The contents of each also vary slightly. But all of them, together with individual verses found in various old anthologies, indicate a continuing Indian interest in Amaru's poetry, stretching over a long time and from many different parts of the country.

A picturesque example of this interest is found in legends that link Amaru with the great Indian philosopher and seer Adi Shankara (c.788–820 AD). That story first appeared[5] in his fourteenth century biography *Shankara Digvijaya* by Madhava Vidyaranya, one of his many followers.

Broadly, it is as follows. As is well known, the sage Shankara travelled all over the country, to propagate and discuss his thoughts. At a discussion in Kashmir he was questioned about erotic matters with which, as a celibate, he was unfamiliar. In order to understand them, using his yogic powers he entered and temporarily brought back to life the just deceased body of the local king Amaru, and visited his harem several times. Thereafter he composed for future record the verses still known by that king's name.

This tale was retold with other embellishments, including in a later Amaru recension, whose editor also considered that the verses had dual meanings, both physical and mystic. But the story has been rejected by modern scholarship over the last century. Also, there is no trace of any king Amaru in the history of Kashmir.[6]

But the work *Amaru Shatakam* itself has always been praised. In present times, this has continued with many famous western scholars. In the words of the respected late Sanskritist A.B. Keith, it is 'essentially a collection of pictures of love . . . gay, high-spirited, delighting in tiny tiffs and lovers' quarrels, but ending in smiles'. The stanzas also 'show the elegance and precision of Amaru's style, and his avoidance of long and difficult compounds'.[7]

Half a century later, another equally respected scholar, A.K. Warder, devoted a whole chapter to Amaru in his multi-volume history of Indian kavya literature. In his words, the 'all-pervading spirit of the Hundred is that of tenderness. There is none of the scepticism or cynicism about love . . . the characters are treated with sensitivity and deep sympathy, especially the women . . . making the work almost unique'.[8]

This appreciation by the western world has continued in recent times. A full translation of *Amaru Shatakam* by Andrew Schelling appeared in Boston as recently as 2004. 'For our times,' Schelling says, 'it shows that long years ago India developed love poetry, original and vivid as that anywhere on the planet.'[9] In the following year, there was a literal rendition by Greg Baily[10] with a roman transcription, both of which have been used for rechecking the present translation.

As far as I know, the last complete and learned translation of Amaru in India, was done by the Sanskrit scholar C.R. Devdhar, about a century ago, and then reprinted in 2014.[11] The time thus seemed ripe to present this new translation in contemporary language for the reader of today, especially in our country where the original was once well known and commented on by famous critics of the time.

While translating it, I also formed some impressions about this celebrated poetic work that I am now glad to present here.

These are ancient lyrics, but they give vivid glimpses of the mutual attraction of men and women in quite a modern manner. The love they picture has physical, emotional as well as social aspects. It is delightful but also painful, and felt by women as much as men. Each verse portrays a different aspect, in simple and direct language. In some cases, there is a continuity of thought in successive verses. In others, the scenes and settings revolve around basic themes, such as union and separation, delight and anger, success and failure. For ease of reading, the presentation here has been divided into seven cantos, each with some shift in its focus. But the overall spirit, that the totality of these verses conveys, appears relevant for all times and places.

This translation is based on the Arjuna Varma Deva recension already mentioned. It has been counter-checked, as also mentioned, with the literal rendition prepared by Greg Baily. In my translation, I have also endeavoured to convey both the spirit and the flavour of the original verses, with the hope that this will give a deeper understanding of our lesser-known Sanskrit poetry to readers of today.

I am grateful to Penguin Random House India and its then editor Ambar Chatterjee for their agreement to my undertaking this translation. My gratitude also to the new editor Ananya Bhatia, and to Tarini Uppal, for their arrangement of this work's editing and publication.

Finally, heartfelt thanks to my wife, Priti, for reading and commenting on several drafts, and to our son, Vikram, for his pertinent suggestions on those that he saw. This has been a work of love, and is now dedicated to my beloved life-companion in this year of our diamond jubilee.

A.N.D.H.
New Delhi
January 2021

My Shameless Heart

Love Lyrics of *Amaru Shatakam*

Benediction

While a bee hovers greedily
near the blossom cluster on her ear,
may the glance of Ambika,
and the glow on her finger nails,
as her hand the bow-string draws
in the manner of an archer—
may all this protect you.   (1)

May the flames of Shambhu's arrows
burn away your sins entire,
like a new lover's misdeed,
when, forcefully grasping the skirt
of a maiden from the triple city,
he holds her hair while bowing down,
that, with her tear-filled lotus eyes,
she does not notice in agitation,
while rejecting his embrace.   (2)

May the face of a slender girl,
hair dishevelled, earrings trembling,
her *tilaka* mark almost removed
by a mist of perspiration,
and eyes languid, after sex
performed upon her partner:
may that face always protect you
what can be done by Hari, Hara,
Skanda, and the other gods? (3)

Canto 1

Your gaze is tender, soft with love,
you shut your eyes repeatedly,
and open them for just a moment
to stare, or shyly dart a glance
full of deep inner feelings.
Say, young lady, who is he,
that lucky man you saw today?   (4)

O Lady, are you angry now,
quietly weeping, wiping tears
all the time, with your finger-tips?
But you will sob and weep much more
when, on some treacherous advice,
your pride becomes excessive, and
despairing of any reunion,
your lover becomes indifferent. (5)

Sir, indeed you gave her love
and pleasure for long,
but, by fate, you did today
something that offended her,
causing an unbearable anger,
that cannot be pacified
by words of conciliation:
and, O iron-hearted man,
you have made my girl-friend weep,
pitifully and profusely. (6)

He who loves you sits outside,
downcast, and scratching the ground;
your famished girl-friends have no food,
their eyes swollen with constant weeping;
and the caged parrots have now ceased
all their laughs and mimicry;
but your state remains the same:
hard-hearted girl, now give up pride.   (7)

Those charming but wicked women
cannot ever be restrained
from stealing your lover boy,
why give up and weep in vain,
why do them a favour?
Handsome, playful, young, good-hearted,
is your husband, timid girl,
he can be won back by you
with just a hundred sweet words,
why use coarse vulgarity? (8)

Tightly held in the bonds, her arms,
soft and tremulous, like a creeper,
that evening, in front of her girl-friends,
she led her love to the bedroom,
hinting at his wicked attempts,
in a sweet but faltering voice,
that 'Once again he thus behaved!'
But that lucky man, denied all this,
and laughed, as she sobbed and struck him.   (9)

'Those who go away on travel,
O beauty, don't they ever meet again?
So, do not worry about me,
you are turning very thin!'
When I said this, tearfully,
then through her eyes, dripping with tears,
and their pupils dulled with shame,
she did laugh and look at me,
in a way that seemed to show
a rash wish for an instant death.   (10)

My face was lowered facing his,
my gaze fixed upon his feet;
I closed my ears, so desperate,
and eager for his words;
with both hands did I try to hide
the signs of thrill and perspiration
that had on my cheeks appeared;
but, O friends, what could I do
when the stitches of my bodice
themselves burst a hundred-fold?   (11)

'Will it be in the night's first phase,
in its middle, or much later,
or when it is completely over,
that, my love, you will return?'
Thus the young girl does delay
her lover's departure for a place
that is a hundred days away.   (12)

At midnight did he hear the sound
of rain pouring from the clouds
and, with a deep sigh and many tears,
thought for long about that girl
from whom he was separated;
then, all night, that traveller wept,
with such loud and bitter wails,
that villagers now forbid way-farers
from spending the night there.   (13)

From a distance, she performed,
with a sweet smile the welcome ceremony.
She bowed her head, when I did speak,
and replied deferentially,
with no slackening in her gaze
thereafter, in my company.
But all of this does burn my soul,
as it is just deception
to hide the wrath pent up within
the heart of this callous woman. (14)

Somehow in a play of pique
I told him to get out, and he,
hard-hearted, just left the bed
and walked away abruptly.
His ardent feelings seem at an end,
but my shameless heart still yearns
for that callous spoiler of our love,
O good friend, what shall I do?   (15)

As the couple chatted
in their bed at night,
their pet parrot heard the words,
and repeated them next morning
in the presence of their elders.
Hearing the bird's shrill tones, the bride,
ashamed, took off her ruby earring,
and, as if it were a pomegranate seed,
put it within the parrot's beak
in order to block its speech.   (16)

Canto 2

You hurt me by humiliating me,
with that inappropriate embrace,
coming at me from behind.
And, O rogue, what did you gain,
by doing this to our life together?
For, do look at your own chest,
coloured with powder rubbed off from
the breast of your sweetheart,
and marked with spots of oil
from her braided hair.   (17)

As he approached her,
she got up in welcome,
leaving no chance for
their sitting together,
avoided his embrace
on the pretext of going
to fetch him a betel leaf,
and did not converse,
keeping busy with servants
in the vicinity.
She was thus courteous
to her lover, but clever
enough to show displeasure.   (18)

Seeing his two girl-friends
upon a single seat,
he crept behind them carefully
and, as if in a game of love,
covered the eyes of one;
then, bending his neck a bit,
that rascal kissed the other
whose cheeks glowed with a laugh within,
as her heart delighted with this love. (19)

She withheld her favour, stopping him
from falling at her feet,
and telling him angrily
that he had hidden what he did:
when that lover went away
she heaved a heavy sigh,
just looking at her girl-friends,
with her hand upon the breast
and eyes awash with tears.   (20)

'Why is that girl with lovely eyes
her skirt so tightly tucked in the girdle,
sleeping once again?'
Thus did the lover softly ask
her attendant, who then said:
'She told me very angrily,
"Mother, he even stops my sleeping!"
and throwing herself on the bed,
has taken this opportunity
to pretend being asleep.'   (21)

When they were in bed together
he took the name of another woman,
and his beautiful partner instantly
turned her face away in anger and aversion,
though he tried to soothe her with sweet words.
But then the lover silent stayed,
and concerned that he felt brushed off,
she quickly turned her neck around
and gazed at him again.   (22)

They were on the same bed,
but lay back to back,
distressed, and they did not speak,
though conciliation with each other
was in the heart of both,
they preserved their dignity.
Then, gradually, the couple turned
their eyes on one another:
their quarrel gone, and with a laugh,
they embraced once more.   (23)

'Let us see, what she does to me,'
and I tried to serious be.
But she thought very angrily:
'Why does he not talk to me?
Is he is so full of roguery?'
In this state, we exchanged glances,
trying to do so stealthily.
I put on a show of laughter,
and she gave up, shedding a tear.   (24)

Her pride and anger had now faded,
those hands now held her moon-like face,
but I had no other means
than to bow down at her feet;
then, suddenly she raised her hands,
like two flags, to cover her eyes,
and a tear fell on her breast,
as the signal of her favour.   (25)

'Your chest bears marks of her embrace,
with paint that was on her breasts,
and which now you try to hide
by an act of such deception
as bowing at my feet.'
'Where are they?' did I then say,
and, to have them fast ignored,
caressed her passionately
so that, her pleasure thus aroused,
she forgot about it.   (26)

'Bewitching girl, without your blouse
you are lovely, you can steal hearts.'
Thus did the girl-friend speak to her
as she was its knots untying
with a smile and joyful eyes,
while she sat on the edge of the bed;
but then, suddenly on some excuse,
she quietly slid away. (27)

Even though her brows contract,
she still does look expectantly;
even though she does not speak,
her troubled face still has a smile;
her beauty may have harsh become,
but her body thrills:
how could she carry on this way,
when that person comes?   (28)

It was the first time that her husband
had committed such a sin,
but, without some friend's advice,
that girl was unaware of signals
sent by a flurry of words and limbs,
so all that she could do was weep
from her lotus-like eyes, with tears
trickling down her cheeks.   (29)

Well, my dear, I do now know
this talk is futile and should stop;
so, go away, it's not your fault,
our fate has turned against us.
If your love, that was so deep,
has now reached this state,
my life too, that was exciting,
has now wilted with pain.   (30)

Canto 3

On your breast a necklace jingles,
on round hips, a girdle tinkles,
gems clink in anklets on your feet,
if you thus go, O charming girl,
to your lover, with beating drums,
why then do you look around,
and tremble as if with some fear? (31)

O Cloud, the southern breeze is gone,
the jasmine's fragrance has diffused,
and summer is over.
Perhaps you can encourage and,
bring back here that loveless man,
who owns cows and has much wealth:
but what is it to me?   (32)

Every morning, when you came,
sleep did leave my eyes,
my sense of tiredness disappeared,
and freshness took its place.
What else has been caused by you?
Even from the fear of death
I have now been freed.
But, you are still in some depression,
and what I'll do for its removal,
that you will just hear. (33)

She is young, my mind is bashful,
she's a woman, I'm so timid;
her breasts are a blooming pair,
and I am with depression filled;
with heavy hips does she prevail,
while I am unable to move;
my fault lies in lack of skill
in dealing with such a person,
that I survive is a real wonder.   (34)

My bangles had been taken off,
and tears did flow incessantly.
Dear friends, momentary was my resolve,
for my heart, to follow him, decided,
when that lover did choose to leave,
and all things left with him.
O my love, if you must go,
why leave your friends behind?   (35)

When that bud, her lower lip
was bitten, and the girl felt fear,
waving a finger, she then spoke
angrily, her eye brows dancing:
'Don't do this, let me go, you rogue!'
But he, who kissed that haughty girl,
had by then obtained the nectar
for which were the oceans churned
by the foolish gods.   (36)

'Friend, he sleeps, and you too should.'
My girl-friends did then say,
but as they left, in some time
when, captured in a spell of love,
with passion did I put my mouth
on his lips, but knew at once
his skin was bristling, and the rogue
had pretended closing eyes!
I was very embarrassed, but
he merely ignored that,
and proceeded doing just
what was suited to that moment.   (37)

Once anger was just a frown,
mere silence a reprimand,
one made up with an exchange of smiles
and a glance that showed good temper.
But see, that love now seems to be
in some kind of ruin, and,
you simply grovel at my feet,
and wilful do I still remain,
for not yet freed of anger. (38)

'O beauty, give up this silence,
look at me, I'm at your feet.
You've never been so cross before.'
By her husband thus addressed,
she cast a glance from half-closed eyes,
shed many tears, but said not a word. (39)

Her breasts squeezed in a tight embrace,
her skin thrilled, and an overflow
of her juice of love does make
the skirt slip down her lovely hips.
She does whisper in soft tones:
'No! No! Noble One, no more!'
Is she sleeping, even dying,
or she clings and melts within my heart?   (40)

As to her gown her husband clings,
she modestly bows her head,
he looks for a strong embrace,
she gently draws her limbs away.
She cannot explain it, but
a glance towards her smiling friend,
shows a new bride's shyness
on this first attempt at love.   (41)

The problem did not disappear
by the loved one's conciliation,
that did great effort need
with many kind-hearted words;
and a long and difficult day,
was somehow endured.
But then their glances came together,
looking at each other's face,
they both laughed, and did forget
all egoistic thoughts and pride.   (42)

Canto 4

Our ties of love now do seem gone,
his respect for them has disappeared,
and so too have his gentle feelings,
he now walks about before me
just like any other man:
and, dear friend, my days do pass
in thinking of this all the time,
I do not know the reason why
my heart breaks not in a hundred pieces.　　(43)

Both had been separated long,
and their limbs were weak with longing,
but as they now greeted each other,
their world became all new:
somehow did that long day pass,
and as the night then came upon them,
their mutual talk went on so long,
that love-making there was none. (44)

A greeting garland did she make,
with her glances, not blue lilies,
and arranged a bed of flowers
with her smiles, not jasmine blooms;
then, for the welcome ceremony,
she gave no water from a jar,
just perspiration of her breasts:
thus that slim girl used her body
for welcoming her darling.   (45)

When that lover was cursed to go away,
but changed appearance and returned,
in confusion I hugged him.
And, dear friend, did say in secret
that to be with him I yearned.
He then said and loudly laughed:
'That is difficult, simple girl!'
By that rogue I am thus cheated,
at this hour of night. (46)

Unsure of my bow to them,
she does with her garment's hem,
cover her feet respectfully,
coyly hides the smile she has,
while not looking straight at me,
then, as I speak, she starts to talk
with her girl-friend separately:
that young girl is full of love,
but delightful also in her pride.   (47)

All the false, disagreeable things
that her friends to her recounted,
she quickly did repeat before
her husband who had been at fault.
But thereafter she behaved,
as the god of love desires:
innocence is the jewel innate
of love, and this its charming way. (48)

He came eagerly from afar,
but was admonished roundly,
and then turned away;
his embrace did flush her face,
with eyebrows arched in anger,
but as he then at her feet did bow,
that proud woman looked down tearfully:
Oh, her eyes have now become
clever to show her lover's guilt.   (49)

'You simple girl,' her husband asks,
'how come, your body is so thin?
Is there a reason, or by chance,
your face and temples too are pale?'
'It's all because of my own nature,'
that slim woman says, and turns away,
as she sighs and a flood of tears
keeps pouring down her eyes.   (50)

The earth shook, and I did tremble,
with my head bowed, trying to speak
and say something to my dear girl.
Embarrassed, I was fated then
to write some lines that may explain
one conclusion in clear terms:
that every maiden has the right
to the form of her own body.   (51)

Then she understood my words,
and cheeks gleaming with a red glow,
in a voice now filled with sobs,
'O how strange this is,' she cried,
her utterance all choked with tears,
as she angrily stamped her foot,
like some weapon, on my head.   (52)

O you hard-hearted woman,
give up these untrue suspicions—
it is not right, with wicked words,
to put this man in misery.
Or, if this is what you have today,
my love, decided as the truth,
then do to me what pleases you,
and will make you feel happy.   (53)

At night, as rain-filled clouds did rumble,
a tearful traveller, missing his love,
declared his deep distress and grief
at a journey meant to benefits bring;
sadly then did people give him
the water-offering of respect. (54)

Drunk with wine, when she did see
on me scratches her hands had made,
she got jealous, began to leave;
'Where are you going?' I then said,
holding that girl's garment sash,
but, face turned away, she cried:
'Let me go! O let me go!'
as her lips throbbed angrily,
what she said, I can't forget.   (55)

What did you get by being
so fickle and self-willed?
He came to your house,
fell at your feet so lovingly,
and you ignored him!
Now you'll never be happy
and weep lifelong,
reaping the fruit of anger.   (56)

'Young woman!' *My lord!* 'Do not be angry!'
What have I done in anger?
'I am hurt. What was my fault?'
Sir, all the faults were mine!
'Then why do you thus weep and sob?'
In front of whom am I doing so?
'Isn't it me?' *What am I to you?*
'My darling!' *I'm not! So I weep.* (57)

Canto 5

'I did not embrace my husband,
why was I such a fool?
He kissed me, and I bowed my face;
why do that, not look at him?'
Thus does a new bride worry,
saying nothing to anyone.
But the young woman feels regret
as she learns the taste of love just born.   (58)

Even when I hear his name,
all my limbs do thrill,
on seeing the moon, his face,
my body like a moonstone glows.
When my husband comes, and then is
close enough to be embraced,
my worries of honour disappear,
while earlier they were adamantine.   (59)

On his forehead, streaks of scarlet paint,
mark of a bangle on the throat,
on his face, some black of *kajal,*
and near eyes, red betel stains:
for a long time, in the morning,
did that doe-eyed woman gaze
at these marks of passion on her lover,
as she sighed and with a lotus played.   (60)

With tears flowing from their eyes,
with promises, as they bow down,
and nice words do such poor women
try to stop their spouses going away:
'It is a bright, auspicious day,'
they say, 'your departure is at dawn.
Go, dear one, what more can I say,
that you'll hear as you do leave.'   (61)

She did not cling to his garment's hem
with her slender arms;
nor did she stand in the doorway,
or herself fall at his feet
and utter the words, 'Just stay!'
But, at a time dark with gathering clouds,
as that rogue prepared to leave,
that slender woman stopped her lover
with what seemed like a river of tears.   (62)

My girl-friends I can trust no more,
nor indeed that person, who
knows the core of my desire.
I cannot even look at him
because of my embarrassment.
People too are clever at
making fun of others,
and skilled in catching subtle hints.
But passion's fire burns my heart,
mother, to whom can I go?   (63)

When my lover comes and says
sweet things, then I do not know,
how I become all eyes to see him,
and all ears to hear his voice.   (64)

'Standing here weighed down with worry,
just looking at you alarms me;
how has your person thus become,
when the grace of your temperament,
O beauty, is its ornament?'   (65)

This question, her lover asked,
but, self-conscious and confused,
she somehow held back her tears,
and 'It is nothing!' said the bride;
whatever he may have done,
how could she describe it?   (66)

My lord, separation is a problem,
desire makes the body thin,
and everyone is in the hands
of pitiless death that counts the days;
so, at least think of one's sense of pride,
how can a woman, soft as a bud,
carry on and live like this?   (67)

'He is, since long, to you devoted,
why ignore him, simple girl?
Lovers are sometimes slow to start,
is that a fault, or an obstacle?'
So did a close friend speak to her,
and that softened her anger,
but suddenly she burst in tears
that would neither stop nor flow.   (68)

In the beginning were the days
when you and I were one.
Then you my loved one, and I was
just a mistress losing hope.
Now you are husband, I the wife,
what more is there to say?
My faith has turned as hard as rock,
this is the fruit I reap today. (69)

'You simple girl, do you intend
to be so naive all the time?
Compose yourself, and mind your honour,
don't be artless with your lover.'
Thus advised by friends, the maid,
with a timorous look replies,
'Hush! Softly! My life's lord may hear you,
he is here, within my heart.'   (70)

'Where are you going, pretty maid,
in this dark of midnight?'
Where lives that person, dear to me,
even more than life.
'Are you not afraid, my girl
of setting forth alone?'
One who carries feathered arrows,
that god Kama goes with me. (71)

Canto 6

His lips were bitten fearlessly
by another girl, who playfully
also struck him with a red lotus,
whose filaments did trouble his sight
so that, he stood with his eyes shut,
as she, with a smiling moon-like face,
stayed there, blowing air on them.
Then confused, or just a rogue,
he did not bow, but kissed her hard.   (72)

'My heart is about to burst,
my body wasted with desire,
friend, I have no use any more
of a lover with love so transient!'
Her words were filled with passion,
but born of pride and anger,
as that doe-eyed girl gazed constantly
towards her lover's path.   (73)

'So much of sandal powder
got rubbed off in our deep embrace
and is scattered on the bed,
that it has now become too rough
for your delicate limbs,' he said.
Then he placed me on his chest,
was aroused and kissed me deeply,
and using his toes like pincers,
that rogue pulled off my garment
as he did what he had wished.   (74)

Her lover's response was long awaited,
but there was a slip in what he said;
and the woman, wan in separation,
was also clever and pretended
that she did not hear him.
But worrying that his words might reach
the ears of some intolerant friends,
she was relieved to find the house empty.   (75)

She looked as far as she could see
at her lover's path, despondently.
The road was bad, the day had ended,
and darkness had begun to spread:
the traveller's wife then took a step
towards their house, but at that moment
thought that he may be coming back,
and quickly turned to see again.   (76)

Her loved one having returned,
she had hundreds of desires,
and somehow the day did pass;
but when they to the bedroom went,
stupid servants kept on talking.
Her heart desperate for sex,
'I've been bitten!' that slim girl cried,
and her silk sash waved to turn off the lamp.   (77)

In a garden near the courtyard,
is a mango tree, splendid with blossoms,
on which hover black bees, buzzing
with their mates in lust for the pollen:
and a young girl there, I think,
covers her body with her sash,
as her breasts tremble and she tries
to stifle sounds while she does weep.   (78)

'I am going!' he did say,
when he had gotten all ready:
to this I listened calmly,
but avoided looking at him,
as he walked out, but while so doing,
turned back many times and just stood.
Then I returned to an empty house!
Life is hard, O friends, do stay!
My weeping is deceptive, and
I am fond of living. (79)

You noticed not your love's impact,
nor did your good friends respect,
why do you, O simple woman
now display this angry pride?
With your own hands, you did collect
these fire brands from which do appear
the fierce flames that end a world,
so, now do not in this forest weep.   (80)

On your cheek, is a dot of *kajal,*
that is by your hand removed,
and the nectar of your lips
is absorbed in your sighs,
the tears that trickled on your neck,
now spread upon your breasts:
you are in love with anger,
O thankless girl, not me.   (81)

On seeing no one in their bedroom,
she got up slowly from the bed,
and looked long at the face of her husband,
who pretended being asleep:
quietly she kissed his cheek,
but noting it had thrilled,
she was embarrassed, bowed her face,
as her loved one loudly laughed
and kissed her hard for long.   (82)

As a rival seemed to be suggested,
she shook her head, with eyebrows raised,
and, on seeing her behaviour,
he bowed to her and stood abashed;
then, on gazing at her face,
her cheeks flushed and red with anger,
he did fall before her feet:
even in the parents' presence,
neither gave up right behaviour.   (83)

I did not long for a dalliance,
had no quivering of the breasts,
no drops of sweat upon the face,
nor a bristling of the body,
till that rogue appeared today;
he is my life's love, steals my heart,
and removes my fortitude,
how can I be proud before him?   (84)

She looked at him with timid eyes,
entreated him with folded hands,
then grasping his garment's sleeve,
embraced him without excuse:
but when that rogue ignored all this,
and dryly prepared to go,
she did then renounce this lover,
who had been dearer than her life.   (85)

The heart of my beloved darling
is burning in separation's fire,
and on the pale slope of her breasts
tear-drops are now trickling down
from her sad eyes, that are fixed
at the path on which I went away.   (86)

His mind full of worry, pain and fear,
wished rejection to avoid,
silently, he fell at her feet,
as he was now ready to leave.
She too felt ashamed, and tired
of this constant agony,
with tears were overcome her eyes
and her bosom heaved with sighs,
for long she looked at her lover,
to stop with all hopes their life together.   (87)

Canto 7

She had suffered in separation,
was weary, pale and gaunt,
with her hair all dull and dry.
But, her radiance was restored
the moment I returned from travel.
Then, at our game of love, delightful,
she so proud and lovely looked,
that I did then sip the lips
of that slender-bodied woman,
in ways that I can never describe.   (88)

I am a sweet girl, and available—
that is what men understand
from my anklets; but it is not
our general or typical nature;
for, a woman's inborn treasure
is shyness and modesty;
and knowing this in her own self,
she does get embarrassed soon,
refrains from sex just for the man,
and does leave that lover. (89)

Moving those bud-like hands all over,
she tries to find her clothes,
and then that flower garland throws
at the burning lamp.
She also covers her husband's eyes,
and laughs in some confusion
as their love-making ends,
while that slender beauty looks
at her partner all the time.   (90)

In every house there are young women,
please go now and ask them,
if their boy-friends bow to them,
as does this, your slave!
O you, who are against yourself,
do not give ear to wicked gossip:
men put to pain repeatedly
also lose their taste for love.　　　　(91)

My cheeks are now burning with sighs,
the heart is churned, the body dried,
I cannot sleep, weep day and night,
as my loved one's face is here no more.
When I disregarded him,
as he bowed down at my feet,
friends, what quality within my self,
then made me angry with my lover? (92)

If, beginning from today,
due to pride or something else,
I say again some words about
my lover and his roguish heart,
then the moonlit night, without him,
will loudly laugh at me,
and the day turn dark with clouds,
as it does in the rainy season.   (93)

'Dearest, this is black!' *So, what?*
Black, but my body is white!
'I will go.' *I too am going.*
'It will be by this path.' *So, be it.*
'O friend, once he did follow for long
the pathway to my heart,
but now he is another person,
who indeed can know a man?'   (94)

Bows at my feet, intimate gossip,
flattering words that steal the heart,
a tight embrace of my slim body,
and a forceful kiss:
this may be a moment's pride,
that I cannot understand,
but I do love this mate of mine,
so, what can I now do?   (95)

That slender woman held back tears
in the presence of her parents,
and they fell on the flame of love
lit within her by separation;
it seems the fumes that then appeared
were emitted from her mouth
as anxious sighs that did distract
a line of hovering bees.   (96)

For long I knit my brows to frown,
and practiced shutting the eyes,
carefully learned how not to laugh,
and to maintain silence;
I even stilled the mind, to gain
composure and calm:
I did all this my pride to guard—
it's success does on fate depend. (97)

He took me to a lonely spot,
saying: 'I must tell you something.'
And I did sit close to him,
with feelings hidden in my heart.
Then he whispered in my ear,
as he grasped my braid,
and did kiss me on the mouth,
as I too, friend, did seize his lips.   (98)

Separated by many lands
and hundreds of rivers, too,
also forests full of hills,
he knows well that his beloved
cannot come before his eyes,
in spite of all efforts;
but standing tiptoe, neck upraised,
and wiping his tears,
that traveller does look again,
thinking of her all the time.   (99)

Love filled his heart on seeing her,
some way to meet was on his mind;
and as passion intensifies,
the need for another maid, to act
as the go-between increases;
but just the thought of deep embraces
does give pleasure to that man,
as he moves around the loved one's house.   (100)

When to the bed my lover came,
my skirt knot opened by itself—
I held the string, but the dress slipped off
with just a bit left on my hips.
That is all I know, dear friend,
for when he took me in his arms,
who was he and I myself,
or how we two made love together,
I don't at all remember.   (101)

'She is here, within the house,
in all other places too is she,
before me and also behind,
on all the paths, and in this bed.'
So feels the man suffering separation,
'O heart,' he says, 'there is no one else,
for me in all this world, but she.
What is all this talk, about
advaita? It is unity.'   (102)

Some Appended Verses

At some place, marked by betel-juice,
at another, dark with burnt incense,
also stains of powder spilt,
or of lacquer foot-prints,
is that bed-sheet; in its folds
are faded flowers from her hair:
all show that woman did make love
in many kinds of postures.   (107)

The household's parrot gently chatters,
'Give me food, for otherwise,
I will loudly speak about
what you did so secretly.'
The new bride dips her face in shame,
but does smile within herself,
like a newly blossomed lotus
fluttering in the breeze.   (117)

The day is preferable to the night,
the night is better than the day,
but, in the absence of my darling,
both indeed just pass away. (125)

O you girl with lotus eyes,
if your heart is filled with anger,
what is left there for your lover?
Then, return the deep embraces
and the fervent kisses that
I had earlier given you.   (133)

My wayward eyes may flit and roam,
this girdle slip, this bodice rip
with the heaving of my breasts,
but, friend, I will not speak again
to that rogue lover, even when
with wounded pride, my heart,
does not then just burst apart.   (146)

If you choose to have no feeling,
then why appear so curious?
If you wish to silent stay,
then why this quivering of your lips?
If your mind seeks meditation,
why does the body bristle with thrills?
If all this is just a show of pride,
then favour me, and give it up.   (149)

If it is certain that you must go,
why the hurry, at least wait
for some more moments, while
I may still look at your face.
Living in this world is like
water flowing down a drain,
who knows if we will meet again?   (163)

Notes

Introduction

1 M. Winternitz, *History of Indian Literature, vol. 3*, Prague 1922; translated into English by Subhadra Jha, Motilal Banarsidass Publishers, Delhi 1967. The author's name is also spelt differently in some texts as Amaruka. But all modern scholars mentioned here, except the one at number 8 below, have kept it as Amaru.

2 A.B. Keith, *A History of Sanskrit Literature*, Oxford University Press, London 1961.

3 N.R. Acharya (ed.), *Amaru Shatakam* (with commentary by Arjuna Varma Deva), Nirnaya Sagar Press, Bombay 1964 (a book entirely in Sanskrit).

4 Keith, *A History of Sanskrit Literature*.

5 Winternitz, *History of Indian Literature*.

6 Keith, *A History of Sanskrit Literature*.

7 Ibid.

8 A.K. Warder, *Indian Kavya Literature, vol. 3*, Motilal Banarsidass Publishers, Delhi 1977.

9 Andrew Schelling, *Erotic Love Poems from India*, Shambala Library, Boston 2004.

10 Greg Baily, Love Lyrics (Clay Sanskrit Library), New York University Press, New York 2005.

11 C.R. Devdhar (ed. & tr.), Amaru Shatakam, Motilal Banarsidass Publishers, Delhi 2014. Some Amaru verse translations were also included in *The Indian Poetic Tradition*, edited by S. Vatsyayan and V.N. Misra, Y.K. Publishers, Agra 1983.

Verses

References are to the bracketed numbers at the end of each verse.

(1) Ambika is another name of the goddess Parvati, consort of the great god Shiva in the Hindu trinity.

(2) Shambhu is another name for the god Shiva in note (1).

(3) *Tilaka* refers to a spot of colour on the forehead that many Indian women still apply. Hari, Hara and Skanda are other names respectively of the Hindu trinity gods Vishnu and Shiva, and the latter's son, Kartikeya.

(7) A verse said by a woman to her girl-friend.

(30) By a man to his mistress.

(36) A reference to Hindu mythology.

(38) A woman says this to her lover.

(51) & (52) These two verses have a combined meaning and are joined together in the original text used for translation.

(54) This perhaps refers to a custom of offering water to passing travellers.

(56) Said by one girl-friend to another.

(60) *Kajal* or collyrium is still widely used as a cosmetic for the eyes.

(66) & (67) The second instance of two verses combined as at (51) & (52) above.

(71) Kamadeva, the god of love, was often portrayed with a bow and arrows of desire.

(81) See (60) above for *kajal.*

(94) This verse gives in sequence a dialogue between two lovers. The woman is the first speaker. Her comment in the last four lines is later made to girl-friends.

(96) This verse picture shows strong sighs and nearby bees.

(97) A woman, on protecting herself from a man's advances.

(98), (149) & (163) Words respectively, between two women, a man to a woman, and woman to man.

(102) The literal meaning of the word *advaita* is non-dual, or a single unity. But the word is also the name used for the philosophy of the great sage Adi Shankara. The legend of that sage's association with Amaru is mentioned in the Introduction. Does the word's usage in this verse relate to that legend, is a question for concerned scholars. For this translation, it points to the unity in a couple's mutual love.

ALSO IN PENGUIN CLASSICS

Kama Sutra
A Guide to the Art of Pleasure

Vatsyayana
Translated by A.N.D. Haksar

'A fine new translation'—*Guardian*
'A clear and elegant new translation'—*New York Times*

Treating pleasure as an art, *Kama Sutra* is a handbook covering every aspect of love and relationships. This new edition highlights the work's historical importance as a sophisticated guide to living well. Conveying all the original flavour and feel of this elegant, intimate and hugely enjoyable work, Haksar's clear, accurate translation is a masterpiece of pithy description and a wry account of human desires and foibles.

The Courtesan's Keeper
Samaya Matrika

Kshemendra
Translated by A.N.D. Haksar

'A brilliant, funny, naughty translation'—Lee Seigel

This feast of smiles was put together
giving the secret strategies
and all the tricks of courtesans

One of Kshemendra's finest satires, *The Courtesan's Keeper* is a delightful and rambunctious rendition of the life and times of the courtesan Kankali as she teaches the ways of the world to her ward Kalavati. From the attractive courtesan and her shrewd keeper to the experienced barber and the avaricious trader, the book brings to life the vibrant society of Kashmir Valley a thousand years ago through a host of characters, each drawn in vivid detail. With its terse narrative, directness and economy of style, and fast-paced action, the book is fully suited for the twenty-first-century reader.

Subhashitavali
An Anthology of Comic, Erotic and Other Verse

Translated by A.N.D. Haksar

This selection from the *Subhashitavali*, a celebrated verse anthology compiled by Vallabhadeva in c. fifteenth-century Kashmir, offers a rich variety of erotic poetry and a wealth of lyrical and gnomic verse. One section is given to earthy humour and cynical satire seldom available in English renditions. Also included are invocations and allegories, panegyrics and pen-pictures, sage observations and stark musings. The sweep of these verses is matched by the eclectic array of contributors—from illustrious poets like Vyasa and Valmiki, Kalidasa and Bana to others now mostly forgotten. These verses of jollity and wit, ribaldry and bawdiness, snide sarcasm and wry comment showcase the fact that Sanskrit literature, generally perceived as staid and serious, can also be flippant and fun.

Chanakya Niti
Verses on Life and Living

Translated by A.N.D. Haksar

Chanakya's numerous sayings on life and living—popularized in the wake of his successful strategy to put Chandragupta Maurya on the throne, if legend is to be believed—have been compiled in numerous collections and anthologies over time. This entire corpus was referred to as Chanakya Niti.

These aphorisms, which continue to be recalled and quoted in many parts of India, primarily deal with everyday living: with family and social surroundings, friends and enemies, wealth and knowledge, and the inevitable end of everything. They also advise on the good and bad in life, proper and improper conduct, and how to manage many difficult situations.

A.N.D. Haksar's wonderful translation also places this work into context, showing how these verses have endured in the popular imagination for so long.